The Velvet Thief

Written by Sally Prue
Illustrated by Alan Marks

Published by Pearson Education Limited, Edinburgh Gate, Harlow, Essex, CM20 2JE
Registered company number: 872828

www.pearsonschools.co.uk

Text © Sally Prue 2012

Designed by Bigtop
Original illustrations © Pearson Education Limited 2012
Illustrated by Alan Marks

The right of Sally Prue to be identified as author of this work has been asserted by
her in accordance with the Copyright, Designs and Patents Act 1988.

First published 2012

2022
10 9

British Library Cataloguing in Publication Data
A catalogue record for this book is available from the British Library

ISBN 978 0 435 07625 2

Printed and bound in Great Britain

Acknowledgements
We would like to thank the children and teachers of Bangor Central Integrated
Primary School, NI; Bishop Henderson C of E Primary School, Somerset;
Brookside Community Primary School, Somerset; Cheddington Combined School,
Buckinghamshire; Cofton Primary School, Birmingham; Dair House Independent
School, Buckinghamshire; Deal Parochial School, Kent; Holy Trinity Catholic
Primary School, Chipping Norton; Lawthorn Primary School, North Ayrshire;
Newbold Riverside Primary School, Rugby and Windmill Primary School, Oxford for
their invaluable help in the development and trialling of the Bug Club resources.

Every effort has been made to contact copyright holders of material reproduced in
this book. Any omissions will be rectified in subsequent printings if notice is given to
the publisher.

Contents

Chapter 1

The terrible stink hit Edward as soon as he opened the garden gate.

"I thought you cleaned out the **jakes pit** last month," he said to the huge backside sticking up out of the hole in the ground next to the wall of the house.

Nat Cobbley glared up at Edward through the eye-watering fumes.

"I did," he said sourly. "But your Great Aunt Anne's coming for a visit and your mother wants everything spick and span."

Edward stared at Nat in dismay.

"Great Aunt Anne? Oh, not *again!*"

Nat stopped shovelling foul-smelling stuff out of the pit and leaned dispiritedly on his spade.

"That's what your mother said – and as for your sister, what *she* said nearly burned the dinner to cinders as she was stirring it."

That sounded just like Edward's sister, Bridget.

Nat put a hand to the small of his back and straightened himself up with a groan.

"I'll have to wash after this, as well," he went on, mournfully. "They'll never let me in the Stag, otherwise."

The Stag Inn wasn't fussy about its customers, but Edward had to agree with him. Nat stank enough to clear a whole street, let alone an inn. Edward was having to hold his cap across his face just in case the fumes from the pit dissolved his eyeballs.

"*And* I've already had my summer wash,"
Nat Cobbley muttered, turning back to his work.
He picked up a shovelful of something deeply
revolting and threw it into the barrow beside
him.

"I don't know why anyone ever thought of
putting the jakes indoors. It's not hygienic. People
should have kept to a good old bucket in a shed
at the bottom of the garden."

Edward wasn't sure about that. He could still just remember their old house, where everyone had had to dash out into the rain and snow to shiver in the dark amongst the spiders. Having a little hut built onto the side of the house by the top of the stairs, so that everything dropped straight down into the pit below, was much more convenient.

Well, it was as long as you weren't the one who had to empty out the pit, anyway.

"It's bad for the health, too," grumbled Cobbley, sliding another moist offering into the barrow.

"Having the jakes in the house?"

"No," said Cobbley, sourly. "Washing."

Edward had a lot of sympathy with him there. His mother made him wash himself every other Sunday morning, and surely it was dangerous to get so damp, especially when you had to go and sit in a cold church for a couple of hours afterwards. Dirt, he thought (and all his friends agreed with him) was very warming.

His sister Bridget came bustling out through the kitchen door. Bridget always bustled. She thought it made her seem important.

"Haven't you finished that *yet?*" she demanded.

Nat Cobbley gave her a filthy look.

"Look, do you want a good job done or not?" he asked. "Because if you're happy to have the whole place knee-deep in – "

"Well, just hurry up, will you?" snapped Bridget. "We're baking, and we can't have the door open with all this stink about."

"Baking?" said Edward, hopefully.

"It's all for when Great Aunt Anne comes, so you needn't stand there with your tongue hanging out," Bridget said. "And Nat, you great lard-gut, stop leaning on your shovel and get back to work!"

She trotted off up the path towards the herb beds and Nat threw down his spade in a sudden rage.

"Lard-gut?" he said, outraged. "*Lard-gut?* That does it. I'm off!"

Edward jumped back hastily to avoid being splattered by the falling spade.

"*Off?*" he said. "Off where? You haven't finished cleaning out the pit!"

"No, and I'm not going to, either." Nat was rolling down his sleeves. "No, I'm for the open road again, I am. Better to sleep in a ditch than to be cleaning up other men's – "

"But you can't go back to being a vagrant!" said Edward, in real alarm.

Cobbley put his great fists on his hips.

"And who's to stop me?" he demanded.

"Well ... the constable," said Edward.

"That overfed old meddler? He won't care if I leave town."

"No," said Edward, "but you'll be arrested as soon as you arrive in a new town, won't you? You know no one's allowed on the roads unless they've got work, or a begging licence, and you'll never get one of those because you're not old, sickly, blind, lame, or mad. Everyone will know you're an illegal vagrant straight away. Why, even the travelling minstrels who used to sing in the town have been banned."

Nat was wiping his shoes on the grass.

"I don't want you to think I'm not grateful to your father for giving me a job," he said, "but every man has his pride, and I've had enough of this. I'm going back to a life on the road. I know there are all sorts of laws against it, but I've managed before and I'll manage again."

"You only managed it by pretending to be one of Sir Robert Cecil's spies!"

"Pretending? *Pretending?* Nay, Master Edward, work-shy you may call me, but don't you go casting me as a liar!"

Edward was suddenly ashamed. Nat Cobbley was a great teller of tales, most of which could surely never be true, but Edward could never forget that Nat had saved his life.

"Please don't go," said Edward earnestly. "Father says that anyone found begging without a licence has a hole bored through his ear – "

" – so?" said Nat, grandly. "I shall hang a gold ring from it!"

" – and that people who are found begging after that are hanged."

Nat rubbed his neck nervously.

"*Hanged?*" he echoed.

Edward nodded.

"So *please* don't go, Nat," he said again. "I'm sorry Bridget was rude to you, and I'm sorry you have to dig out the jakes pit, but Great Aunt Anne doesn't come very often. Just think about how old she is: she can't live all that much longer, can she?"

Nat Cobbley grunted.

"That old crone's so sour she must be filled to the ears with vinegar," he said. "She's probably pickled beyond decay."

He looked down glumly at the jakes pit.

"This is no job for a man," he said.

But he picked up the shovel again and, sighing a great sigh, went back to work.

Chapter 2

Great Aunt Anne not only came, but she arrived a whole day early. Edward was sitting on the doorstep plucking a **brace of quails** when he heard the clip-clopping of hooves in the street.

When he looked up at the gate he saw a hefty knobbly-looking woman balanced upon a large sad-looking mare.

"Great Aunt Anne!" he exclaimed.

Nat's head popped up suddenly from behind the pig sty, and there was a flurry of squawking from the kitchen which meant Mother and Bridget must have heard the news, too.

Great Aunt Anne scowled down at Edward.

"Well, come and take my bridle, then, boy!" she snapped. "I've ridden two days to get here and I need rest!"

Edward went forward obediently and discovered that there was a beautiful chestnut horse standing behind the mare. Its rider was a young man with a fashionable little beard. The badge on the sleeve of his velvet doublet showed that he worked for someone very important indeed.

The young man dismounted, gave his reins to Nat Cobbley, and came round to Great Aunt Anne. She smiled at him gratefully as he lifted her down from her mare.

Edward was amazed. He hadn't known that Great Aunt Anne *could* smile.

The young man's horse was rolling its eyes nervously, but Nat Cobbley was a marvel with animals. He put out a hand to give the horse a reassuring pat, but then had to hop quickly aside to avoid the horse's stamping hooves as the beast shied and side-stepped at his touch. The horse was really upset about something.

The young man was too busy smiling back at Great Aunt Anne to notice that his horse was in trouble.

"This is Master Giles Pettit," announced Great Aunt Anne, as she shook out her skirts.

"He's secretary to my Lord of Essex," she went on, with an important nod.

Edward thought he'd better bow. Master Pettit had the sort of face which belongs in an oil painting – it was very handsome, and as pale as marble.

By the time Edward had straightened up, Great Aunt Anne was leading the way up the path to the house, her heavy skirts bouncing over her fashionable **bum roll**.

"Come along, Master Pettit," she was saying kindly. (Kindly? Aunt Anne? *Kindly?*) "My niece will be most pleased to welcome you."

Edward watched them go. This Master Pettit was young, good-looking, important, and, amazingly, Great Aunt Anne liked him.

Nat Cobbley, leading Master Pettit's shivering and reluctant horse to the stables, stopped for a moment to give Edward a meaningful look.

And Edward suddenly realised that Nat had taken as violent a dislike to Master Giles Pettit as Edward had himself.

"Won't you have another **jumble**, sir?" Bridget cooed, offering Master Pettit a **pewter platter**. "I baked them all myself."

Edward was by now totally confused. Bridget had been complaining all week about the extra work Great Aunt Anne's visit was causing, and now Great Aunt Anne had arrived with yet another visitor – a stranger, too – and Bridget was *cooing*. Why, she was even offering the man extra biscuits.

The only explanation Edward could think of was that Bridget had put poison in them.

Great Aunt Anne was beaming round the table at Mother and Bridget. Father was away on business until tomorrow.

"It was such *luck* meeting Master Pettit," she said, "and just when my stupid servant John had decided to go and drop dead like that, too!"

Master Pettit shook his bearded head.

"Servants are so unreliable nowadays," he said, regretfully.

Mother tut-tutted.

"Oh, but to think that you might have had to travel alone, Aunt," she said. "And with all these thieves and vagrants about."

"Well, Master Pettit came to my rescue," said Great Aunt Anne in triumph. "It was very lucky. Master Pettit had been taken ill himself on the road, and my Lord of Essex's business was so urgent that poor Master Pettit had to be left behind all alone at the inn to recover. So we were able to travel together."

Edward looked round at the others. There was something about this Master Pettit that roused his deep distrust, and this story made him even more suspicious. If the man had been alone when Great Aunt Anne had met him, that meant there could be no proof that he was who he claimed to be.

But Great Aunt Anne and Mother and Bridget were looking at Master Pettit with round, admiring, sparkling eyes.

"Well, I'm very glad you're better now, Master Pettit," said Mother, kindly.

"You must rest, though, before you continue your journey," said Great Aunt Anne. "You must stay here for tonight, at least."

Edward looked across at his mother and sister to see how they were taking this dreadful piece of bossiness.

Mother and Bridget were beaming from ear to ear.

Chapter 3

The garden of Edward's house was small. Half of it was taken up with the pigsty, the barn, and the stable. Mother and Bridget still seemed to feel the need to show Master Pettit all round the rest, though. And the way Giles Pettit was admiring it, anyone would have thought it was the Queen's own garden at **Nonsuch Palace**.

"Ah," he said, bending down to inspect some flowers. "Dandelions!"

"You're quite right, Master Pettit," agreed Mother, as if being able to recognise a dandelion was a rare talent. "We use them in **sallets**."

"Daisies, too," put in Bridget, showing off as usual, "and primroses in the spring."

"And here," said Mother leading the way, "are our onions."

"Onions!" exclaimed Master Pettit in amazement, as if Mother had shown him something really extraordinary, like a **potato**.

Edward went off in search of someone more sensible. He found Nat in the stables, talking to Master Pettit's beautiful chestnut horse.

"Steady, lad," he was saying, while the creature rolled its eyes and stamped. "It's all right, now. I may be smelly, but there's no harm in me."

"He's ever so nervous," said Edward.

Nat Cobbley ran a hand over the horse's gleaming neck.

"That he is, poor beast," he agreed. "Something must have upset him, but I can't think what. The mare's all right, and she can be a right awkward beast, just like her mistress. Hey, steady there, steady!"

Edward perched himself on the side of the mare's stall as Nat sat down with a polishing cloth and a tangle of bridles.

Nat stopped in the act of sorting through the various straps and buckles.

"That's funny," he said.

"What?"

"Well, look at the chestnut's bit."

Nat held up the iron bit that went in the horse's mouth to control it.

Edward looked at it.

"It looks just ordinary to me," he said.

Nat nodded.

"That's right. It is."

"Well, so what?"

"Well, Master Edward, I'd expect something more special for a jittery animal like this."

"Perhaps he isn't usually nervous," suggested Edward.

Nat Cobbley looked thoughtful.

"Perhaps he's not," he agreed. Then he looked up at Edward with a bright shrewd eye. "So that leaves us wondering why he's so nervous today," he said. "Doesn't it?"

When Edward got back to the house, he found Bridget showing Master Pettit the silver spoon Grandmother had given her.

Master Pettit turned it over to look at the hallmark.

"It's very fine," he said. "A lovely thing to remind you of your grandmother, Mistress Bridget."

"Oh, and we have her gold cross, too," said Mother, happily, getting up to fetch it.

"Don't forget your garnet brooch, too," called Great Aunt Anne after her. "I'm sure Master Pettit would like to see it."

Master Pettit smiled charmingly at everyone, and Edward felt more worried than ever.

Edward and Bridget always had to sleep downstairs on straw-stuffed sacks when they had guests. That night Bridget nagged on and on about Master Pettit.

"Scowling like that!" she snapped. "Poor Master Pettit. How could he feel welcome?"

"I wasn't trying to make him feel welcome," pointed out Edward.

"But why not? He's so handsome, isn't he? And polite. Why, he's even made Great Aunt Anne almost pleasant."

Edward couldn't explain what was wrong, but he was sure there was something..

"I don't trust him," he said. "You shouldn't have shown him our treasures."

Bridget rolled her eyes.

"He's secretary to my Lord of Essex," she said, slowly, as if to an idiot. "Just think of all the treasures his lordship must have. If Master Pettit wanted to steal something, he could do it from his lordship's house, and most probably no one would even notice."

Then she turned over crossly and went to sleep.

Edward lay awake worrying for a long time. At last he could bear it no more. He got up, took the wooden bucket that was half-filled with water from the well ready for the morning, and went quietly upstairs. He opened Giles Pettit's door just a little and balanced the bucket carefully on top of it.

Then at last he managed to get to sleep.

Edward was woken up by a tremendous banging and clattering. He opened his eyes and blinked round blearily into the darkness.

Beside him, Bridget sat up and gave a short howl.

"I'm sitting in a puddle!" she exclaimed, in outrage. "What's going on?"

Edward hadn't got the faintest ...

... oh.

Edward opened the back door to let in some light. The wooden bucket was rolling gently across the floor in the grey light of the dawn, and there was water dripping down the stairs.

Master Pettit proved to be wet through. By the way everyone fussed over him, anyone would have thought he was made of sugar and at risk of dissolving. Mother gave him Father's best shirt and took Master Pettit's own shirt away to be washed and then thoroughly dried on the bushes.

Great Aunt Anne slapped Edward viciously on the arm. "Wretched boy! How dare you play such monkey tricks on our guest?" she demanded.

"I was worried in case he stole something," explained Edward, rubbing his arm to try to get rid of the sting.

Mother came bustling past with a mop and took the opportunity to slap him too, in a half-hearted sort of way.

"You are foolish, Edward," she said. "You *know* I need you to be a help to me, especially when Father's away."

"But I was *trying* to be a help!" Edward protested – but it was no good. No one would listen. No one would ask Master Pettit what he'd been doing leaving his room in the middle of the night, either, and every time Edward himself opened his mouth to ask, someone told him to be quiet.

Bridget had no sympathy for him at all.

"As if Master Pettit was going to rob us!" she exclaimed, as she cut Edward a chunk of bread to take to school with him for his dinner. He'd usually have had a jumble, too, but they'd given them all to Master Pettit the night before. "You are a *fool*, Edward!"

"Just wait until your father gets home," said Great Aunt Anne. "He'll give you such a hiding!"

Edward stopped off at the stables on the way to school.

"Sounded as if there was a bit of trouble in the house, last night," observed Nat Cobbley.

"Just keep an eye on that Giles Pettit," said Edward, darkly. "One very, *very* careful eye."

Chapter 4

Father's horse still wasn't back in its stall when Edward got home from school.

Giles Pettit's horse was still in the stable, though.

"Pettit? He's gone into town," Nat told Edward. "Dame Anne and Mistress Bridget wouldn't be content unless he went shopping with them."

"Goodness knows why anyone would want to be seen with *him*," said Edward, bitterly.

"Oh, he's good-looking, and he speaks prettily. But Master Edward, look at this."

Cobbley picked up a saddle and turned it towards the light. There was something stamped into the leather of the **cantle**.

Edward peered at it. It was a shield.

"I expect that's my Lord of Essex's coat of arms," he said.

Nat Cobbley gave him a sideways look.

"Well, if it is, it's not the same as the one Master Pettit has on the velvet sleeve of his doublet," he said.

That was odd.

"I'll tell you something else," said Nat. "I'd have expected a beautiful horse like that to be carrying my Lord of Essex himself, and not his secretary."

Edward's eyes widened.

"You think ..."

Nat Cobbley shook his great bearded head.

"Oh, it's not my place to think," he said. "It's my place to sleep over the stable and clean out the jakes pit."

Then he gave Edward a sideways look from his bright eyes and went on: "But if it was ..."

Edward felt a spark of hope.

"What, Nat?"

"If it *was*, then I might notice the address on a letter he asked me to take to a postal rider."

Edward's eyes popped.

"You can *read?*" he said, in amazement.

"Oh, I only went to **petty school**, Master Edward," said Nat, "but the dame who taught us was as sharp as a new needle. My father got good value for every penny he spent on my schooling."

"So who was the letter to?" Edward asked.

"Walter Bagge," said Nat. "I've heard of him. He's an **Upright Man**."

"A what?"

"An Upright Man. A vagabond king."

Edward blinked.

"Vagabonds have *kings?*"

"Oh yes, Master Edward. Anglers, Abraham Men, Priggers of Prancers, they all obey an Upright Man."

Edward knew about Anglers, who stole valuables through the windows of houses by hooking them on long sticks, and Priggers of Prancers, who stole horses, and Abraham Men, who pretended to be mad so people would give them money.

"And this Walter Bagge ...?" he asked, looking thoughtful.

"... is as clever a villain as you'll find in all of England!" replied Nat.

Edward began to smile.

"Then that *proves* it!" he exclaimed. "I knew Giles Pettit was no good. And this proves it!"

"Well, it *would* do," agreed Nat Cobbley. "Except that your great aunt and sister are that dazzled by him, they'll never believe it."

"But we must do something!" exclaimed Edward. "He's probably planning to steal everything in the house!"

"I don't doubt it. And it's easy to see why this poor horse has the wrong badge on its saddle, too, isn't it?"

"Master Pettit's a prigger of prancers!"

"Who's happy to nab a few silver spoons if he gets the chance," said Nat Cobbley, shaking his head. "Villains nowadays, eh? They don't even stick to their proper crimes any more."

"But what can we *do?*" demanded Edward.

Nat Cobbley made a long face.

"Not a lot, that I can see."

"Perhaps we could search his baggage, and –"

"Oh, I've done that. There's nothing there that shouldn't be. He's a cunning rogue."

Edward clenched his fist. Giles Pettit was a thief and there must be some way they could prove it. There *must* be.

"Come on," said Edward, suddenly.

"Come on where?"

"To find Giles Pettit and watch his every move. A man like that will never get around town without stealing something – and then we've *got* him!"

Chapter 5

It wasn't hard to find Great Aunt Anne, at least: her voice, raised in complaint, could be heard from the other side of the square. Edward sidled up to Bridget, who was standing a little way away looking sour.

"Where's Giles Pettit?" he asked.

Bridget turned a disgusted face on him.

"He said he had business to attend to and went off," she said. "I'm not surprised, either. Great Aunt Anne *will* complain about every little thing."

"But so do you," pointed out Edward.

"Not like Great Aunt Anne," said Bridget, swiftly. "I only make comments out of politeness, to show an interest."

Edward grunted.

"Did you see which way Giles Pettit went?"

Bridget hesitated.

"Into the Stag Inn," she admitted, reluctantly.

The Stag: the roughest inn in the town.

"Come on," said Edward to Nat Cobbley.

"You can't go into the Stag!" exclaimed Bridget. "It's not respectable!"

"I'll be all right if Nat's with me."

Bridget looked back towards Great Aunt Anne. She was still explaining to a spice seller the fifteen ways in which his spices were the worst she'd ever seen.

"Great Aunt Anne won't miss me for half an hour," said Bridget. "So I might as well come along too."

"But you're a girl. You can't go – "

Bridget clenched her fists.

"If you don't let me come, I'll scream," she threatened.

She would, too.

"Oh all right," said Edward.

Nat Cobbley ducked through the door of the Stag Inn and Edward and Bridget followed close behind him.

The earthen floor inside was covered in stinking rushes. Bridget wrinkled her nose, but before she could say anything there was an outburst of cheering and booing from a group of men sitting round a table.

Nat led the way quietly over to join them.

Giles Pettit was there, looking quite unlike himself. He'd unbuttoned his velvet doublet and taken off his ruff and he was mopping his brow with his handkerchief. He tucked his handkerchief in his sleeve and then he threw something down on the table. All eyes followed the little tumbling dice.

"Double six!" shouted someone, and there were more cheers and boos. Silver coins were flicked across the table to Giles Pettit, who grinned agreeably as he scooped them up.

Nat Cobbley drew up a stool in a leisurely kind of way and settled himself down to watch.

Nat seemed to enjoy the dice game thoroughly. He didn't join in, but he cheered with the winners, and groaned with the losers, and laughed the loudest of any of them.

He even bought beer for the whole crowd (except for Edward and Bridget, who were only allowed to have ale, as they did at home).

Bridget was the first to get restless.

"Great Aunt Anne will be missing me," she said to Edward.

"Well, you'd best be getting back, then," said Edward, his mind on the game. Giles Pettit wasn't winning every throw, but over the last twenty minutes far more coins had gone into his purse than had been taken out. The man was flushed, and perhaps a little drunk, and he kept having to wipe his face with his handkerchief.

Edward knew that Bridget was right, though. Time was getting on. They'd have to be getting back for supper even though Giles Pettit hadn't said or done anything at all to prove that he was a villain.

Edward nudged Nat Cobbley, who had been watching Giles Pettit's every move with great attention.

"We're going to have to go home," he whispered, unhappily. He was thinking about the beating he would get from his father for putting that bucket of water on Master Pettit's bedroom door. He had long since given up hope of anyone agreeing that *that* had been a good idea.

Nat Cobbley nodded, and swigged the last of his beer. He got to his feet, but paused to watch one last throw of the dice.

It was Giles Pettit's turn again. He pushed his handkerchief back up his sleeve, rubbed the dice between his hands, blew on them, and then scattered the dice with an elegant flick of his thin wrist.

There was a tense silence while the little dice bounced and tumbled – but just before they came to a halt Nat Cobbley's great hand shot out and snatched them up.

There was a moment's astonishment, and then everyone started shouting.

Nat Cobbley grinned round the table.

"Oh, sorry," he said. "Did I spoil the game? I just wanted a go with the magic dice. I was wondering if they work even when Master Pettit doesn't tuck them in his handkerchief first."

And he threw them carelessly onto the table.

Two sixes.

"Ah, they do work!" said Nat Cobbley, with a sigh. "It's a pity I'm not a gambling man, or I could have made a nice little sum just then."

He took up the dice and threw them again.

Two sixes.

The men round the table were staring at the dice as if they couldn't believe their eyes, but Nat Cobbley laughed.

"Beginners' luck," he said, gathering up the dice and throwing them once more.

Two sixes.

The other men were exchanging glances now. Pettit made a grab for the dice, but Nat Cobbley was too quick for him.

Nat Cobbley threw again.

Two sixes.

At last people began to speak:

"They're crooked!"

"He's been hiding the true dice in his handkerchief!"

"That villain's cheated me of seven pence farthing!"

"*Seven pence farthing?* He's taken a shilling from me!"

There was a sudden scuffling, but Nat Cobbley did something with his foot and Giles Pettit was suddenly measuring his length along the floor.

Nat Cobbley put out a huge arm to grab the man, but Giles Pettit squirmed over onto his back and suddenly they all saw the dagger in his hand.

Everyone shouted and then they all went quiet. Giles Pettit got up and stood, crouching slightly, licking his lips and shooting glances round at the others.

"Come any closer, Cobbley, and I'll slit you from throat to navel," he said quietly.

Nat Cobbley didn't go any closer.

"Throw me my cloak," ordered Pettit.

Edward looked at Nat, who nodded, but Bridget was there before him.

"Here we are, Master Pettit," she said respectfully – and then flung the thing right in his face.

Pettit ducked instinctively, and in that moment Nat Cobbley acted. He raised a great arm and chopped down hard on Pettit's wrist so that the dagger flew away, clattered against the wall, and fell down into the grubby shadows.

"Get it!" bellowed Nat Cobbley to Edward as he stepped forward, balanced on his toes ready to fight. A punch from Nat would fell an ox, and Pettit knew it.

"Stay back," Pettit snapped. "You have no right to touch me."

"No?" said Cobbley, sounding disappointed. "Well, I suppose you are a sort of royalty if you're a friend of Walter Bagge."

Giles Pettit's eyes flickered at the mention of the Upright Man.

"I don't know what you're talking about," he said. "I'm secretary to my Lord of – "

"Of course, you are," said Nat Cobbley. "That's why your horse's saddle is stamped with someone else's badge."

There was a growl from the other men, and someone called out, "Don't let him get away with my money, Nat!"

Pettit licked his lips again.

"Lies," he said. "All lies. I know no Upright Man. I know nothing of those dice, either. Did I throw sixes all the time, as he did? This great oaf must have swapped them."

Cobbley shook his head sadly.

"Now, why should I do that?" he asked. "I've not been playing today – and these fine fellows know why."

The other men laughed, and someone said, "If Nat's got weighted dice then they're weighted on the wrong side, because he only ever throws ones and twos!"

Cobbley chuckled, too, but his eyes were watchful.

"I've never been a gambler," he admitted. "I've got no talent for that at all. But as for fighting ..."

He swung a huge fist, and Pettit ducked and threw himself towards the doorway. Edward tried to block Pettit's path, but Pettit pushed him violently aside. By the time Edward had untangled himself from the stool he'd fallen over, Pettit had disappeared and all the others were piling out through the doorway after him.

Nat could move fast for such a big man, but Pettit might have got away up Gum Alley if a horseman hadn't been emerging from the narrow street and blocked it.

Nat rushed forward, but Pettit dodged round him like an eel, jabbed his elbow viciously into Nat's vast gut, and might have escaped him if Nat hadn't slipped on some rubbish, caught hold of Pettit's doublet as he fell, and brought Pettit down with him.

Edward stood watching, his mouth open with wonder. He suddenly realised that this was the best thing that had happened for ages. Possibly the best thing ever.

Pettit was rolling and kicking and trying to stop Nat Cobbley getting on top of him. Nat was much the heavier, though, and it was looking as if the fight wouldn't last long when Pettit's foot made vicious contact with Nat's ankle bone.

Nat howled like a dog and Pettit wriggled clear and then to his feet.

Several of the other men threw themselves forward to stop him, but all they managed to do was crash into each other. Bridget did manage to catch hold of Pettit's sleeve, but Pettit gave Bridget a great shove which pushed her into a passing old lady (oh no, that was Great Aunt Anne). Then he dodged neatly under the belly of the horse that'd just emerged from Gum Alley – and found himself caught by the collar.

"Not so fast, sir," said the horseman, reprovingly, holding on tightly to the squirming man. "There seem to be people here who wish to speak to you."

"He's a cheat!" called several voices. "Hold him!"

"Father!" shouted Edward and Bridget.

"Nephew!" exclaimed Great Aunt Anne.

In no time at all Giles Pettit had been seized by many hands, turned upside down, and shaken until his pockets were empty.

"My silver scissors!" cried Great Aunt Anne.

"That's my purse!" snapped Bridget, snatching it up.

By that time, the old constable and Alderman Coote had puffed along and put Pettit firmly under arrest.

The landlord of the Stag Inn came out with a tankard of beer and thrust it into Nat's hand.

"That's for fighting the villain outside in the street, and not wrecking my parlour," he said.

Nat swallowed the beer in a single swig. Then he wiped the dust from his sleeve and the sweat from his brow, and began to laugh.

"You were brilliant, Nat!" said Edward, his eyes shining.

"Oh, it was nothing," said Nat Cobbley, accepting another tankard of beer.

"That's for getting me my shilling back," said the man who gave it to him.

Nat finished that one off happily, too.

Father was dismounting from his horse.

"I suppose it's too much to ask why you're brawling in the street, Nat, instead of doing your work?" he asked, mildly.

"It's a long story," said Edward. "That man is a dreadful villain, isn't he, Great Aunt Anne?"

Great Aunt Anne gave him a perishing look – but then she sighed.

"It seems he is," she said. "It seems he is."

Nat Cobbley finished his beer and threw his arm round Edward's shoulders. Nat was beaming, as happy as Edward had ever seen him, despite not being completely steady on his feet.

Suddenly, Nat Cobbley began to sing.

"Of Watking's ale I took a pull
And now have drunk my belly full."

Edward winced. Nat's voice was rich and sweet, but it was loud to have booming straight into your earhole.

Nat Cobbley hadn't finished, either. He took in a deep breath and sang even louder.

"The proverb old, as I do think,
Such ale is brewed, such must I drink!"

Then he stopped, and bowed so magnificently that if Edward hadn't been holding him he would certainly have fallen over.

Alderman Coote was regarding Nat thoughtfully.

"Isn't this the man who helped with that rascal schoolmaster?" he asked Father.

"Indeed he is," said Father, with a sigh. "He's a good man at heart, but ... noisy, I'm afraid."

Alderman Coote nodded his head.

"So tell me, my man," he said to Nat. "Now I have heard you sing, I think I know you. Were you not one of those travelling minstrels I saw so often at Sir Robert Cecil's house?"

"You were a travelling minstrel?" said Bridget, amazed. Travelling minstrels were much missed by everyone since so many of them had been banned because they were too much like vagrants and vagabonds.

Nat Cobbley sighed.

"Aye, I was," he said. "That was the way I earned my bread before I sank to being a digger-out of jakes pits."

Edward was filled with amazement, too. Nat had been at Sir Robert Cecil's house! Sir Robert Cecil, master of all the Queen's spies – and no one, Edward suddenly realised, would be a better spy than a minstrel, who could go anywhere.

So did that really mean that *Nat Cobbley ...?*

Alderman Coote rubbed his hands together.

"Then I have a new job for you, Nat," he said. "The constable here is a good man, but he is old. He cannot run as fast as he once could. Not only that, but we all miss the music the minstrels used to bring to the town. I think I shall start a band of waits, and you shall be its captain."

Nat Cobbley stared at the alderman for a long time.

"A **wait**?" he said hoarsely. "I'd be a night watchman for the town, and fight villains, and sing for Christmas and May Day, and in all the town processions?"

"Yes, my good man. Will you take on the job?"

Cobbley was suddenly grinning so widely that Edward could see all the gaps where his teeth had been knocked out.

"Fighting villains and singing?" he cried joyfully. "Why, of course, your honour. That is a job for a MAN!"

Edward turned over in his bed. It was the middle of the night, and there was rain pattering on the window.

Streets away, someone was singing.

"Past three o'clock,
On a mild and rainy morning.
Past three o'clock,
Good morrow, masters all!"

Then there was the clattering of a shutter opening, and someone shouted: "Hold your peace, you great fat fool! Some of us have to work tomorrow!"

Edward smiled to himself and went back to sleep.

Glossary

brace of quails pair of small birds killed by hunting

bum roll long cushion worn below the waist for giving shape to a lady's skirts

cantle raised curved part at the back of a horse's saddle

jakes pit trench beside the wall of a house, which caught toilet droppings

jumble biscuit

Nonsuch Palace palace with a famous garden, built by Henry VIII

petty school school for young boys, often run by a local housewife in her home, where they learned to read and write English

pewter platter serving plate made from a mix of tin and lead

potato potatoes were first brought from Peru to England during the reign of Elizabeth I

sallets vegetable dishes

Upright Man skilled, professional thief, who had authority over other beggars

waits musicians employed by the town council who had various other duties, too